HOW TO READ THE BIBLE "LITERALLY"

– AN ILLUSTRATED GUIDE –

....

WRITTEN, DESIGNED, AND ILLUSTRATED BY

BILL FOSTER

First printing: August 2017

New Leaf Press, P.O. Box 726, Green Forest, AR 72638

New Leaf Press is a division of the New Leaf Publishing Group, Inc.

ISBN: 978-0-89221-756-4
ISBN: 978-1-61458-627-2 (digital)
Library of Congress Number: 2017949561

Cover design & book layout:
Bill Foster / Bill Foster Design / www.billfosterdesign.com

Please consider requesting that a copy of this volume be purchased by your local library system.

Printed in the United States of America

Please visit our website for other great titles:
www.newleafpress.com

For information regarding author interviews,
please contact the publicity department at (870) 438-5288.

New Leaf Press
A Division of New Leaf Publishing Group
www.newleafpress.com

CONTENTS

WHAT DOES **LITERALLY** MEAN?

Skeptics and theological liberals often ridicule Christians as simpletons for reading the Bible "literally." This section will illustrate how understanding the true meaning of "literally" provides the only informed way of reading Scripture.

William Dever, archaeologist and consultant for the NOVA production, *The Bible's Buried Secrets,* states the following:

....

"It's a waste of time to argue with fundamentalists. And this film doesn't do it. It's designed for intelligent people who are willing to change their mind. And of course, one film is not going to change religious life in America, but it will give intelligent people who want to read the Bible in a modern way a chance. If we insist on reading the Bible **literally**, in 25 years nobody will read it any longer." [1]
(emphasis mine)

....

Comments like this suggest that evangelicals robotically absorb every biblical word in a one-dimensional, wooden fashion while "intelligent people" read it with sophistication in a "modern way."

However, it is not secular interpretations of science nor 21st-century social sensibilities that determine how the Bible should be read.

It is the *intent of the author* that determines how the Bible – or any other written work – should be read:

"LITERALLY"

SKEPTIC'S
MEANING

Simplistic, wooden

ACTUAL
MEANING

What the **author** intended

So to read "literally" means that a passage can be read *both figuratively and straightforwardly* – whichever meaning the author intends.

At the 38th Annual Kennedy Center Honors, orchestral conductor Seiji Ozawa was praised with the following introduction to his lifetime of achievement:

"Seiji Ozawa's devotion to the score and his **ability to divine what the composer intended** are at the heart of his success in bringing classical music alive for new audiences." [2]

Classical symphonies are masterpieces created by truly brilliant composers. Ozawa's conducting skill in exhibiting those composers' original brilliance – rather than putting his own interpretative spin on them – is what has allowed classical music to be appreciated by contemporary audiences.

We should take the same care in preserving the original intent of Scripture so that its supernatural brilliance can be appreciated today. Unfortunately, not everyone looks at Scripture this way. Comedic actor Jim Carrey made the following revelation:

"I discovered a new thing in the Lord's Prayer that kind of hit me," Carrey says. "'On earth as it is heaven' **to me** means whatever you take out into the world is what you're going to draw out. Like those days when you're all yang and no yin..." [3]

By using the "to-me" reading method, Jim Carrey stands the Lord's Prayer on its head. He completely reverses the point of the prayer, which is to model for us how to seek the will of God in heaven *above* – not heaven *within* – to determine our direction here on earth.

Carrey's reading is a classic example of biblical **eisegesis** – *reading into* the Bible according to one's own preconceived notions.

Never qualify the meaning of a Bible verse by using "to me." Our personal take on a passage's meaning is irrelevant (although its *application* may be very relevant). Instead, we should read *out of* the Bible the meaning the author intended us to receive. This is **exegesis**.

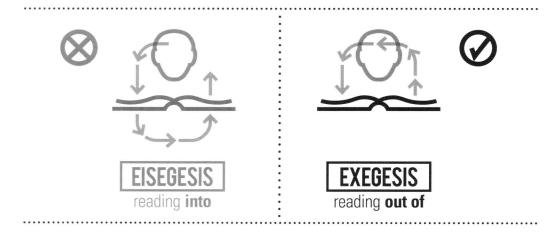

EISEGESIS
reading **into**

EXEGESIS
reading **out of**

The big problem with reading *eis*egetically is that doing so allows each verse to have *multiple meanings*. However, this would mean that if the author had multiple meanings in mind for the audience of that day, then they would have been very confused.

An important principle to remember is that **each verse has:**

To illustrate that each verse has one meaning with multiple applications, here is an example in which Jesus' answers the question of the legality of divorce:

But from the beginning of creation, *'God made them male and female.'* — Mark 10:6 (emphasis mine)

MEANING: Despite the trivialized views of divorce held by different religious schools at the time, God's design for man and woman since the beginning is a one-flesh, lifelong union, not divorce.

APPLICATION #1: Although Jesus never explicitly said that homosexuality was wrong, He implied it by citing how God designed man and woman for a complementary, one-flesh union.

This is a commonly cited application of Mark 10:6, but there is another application that emphasizes the first part of the verse:

> But *from the beginning of creation*, 'God made them male and female.' — Mark 10:6

APPLICATION #2: Jesus understood human beings to be made *at the beginning* of creation, not at *the end* of a multi-million-year process as evolutionists and old-earth advocates believe.[4]

In our everyday communication, no one expects each sentence we write or say to have multiple *meanings,* so why should we read the Bible that way? However, we should expect the "living word" (Heb. 4:12) to *apply* to all people of all times in all manner of human experience.

5 KEY QUESTIONS

AND HOW TO APPLY THEM TO SCRIPTURE

WHERE AM I?

The first thing we should recognize when interpreting a biblical passage is where we are in the Bible itself (i.e., what kind of literature/genre we are reading). To illustrate this concept of literary location, we will diagram the Bible as if it were a city.

Suppose the Bible were a city named *Bibliopolis,* consisting of five boroughs or sectors of interconnected streets and blocks, each with its own style:

 ## THE LAW [GENESIS-DEUTERONOMY]

Writing Style – *Prose Narrative* (ordinary language that records historical events in the order they occur) plus occasional *Poetry* by people within the accounts

Purpose – Record the foundations of humanity and trace the patriarchs of Israel from Abraham to Joshua

....

 ## HISTORY [JOSHUA-ESTHER | 4 GOSPELS & ACTS]

Writing Style – *Prose Narrative*

Purpose – [JOSHUA-ESTHER] Record the history of the nation of Israel [4 GOSPELS & ACTS] Describe the life of Christ and the spread of the gospel by early church planters (apostles) such as Peter and Paul

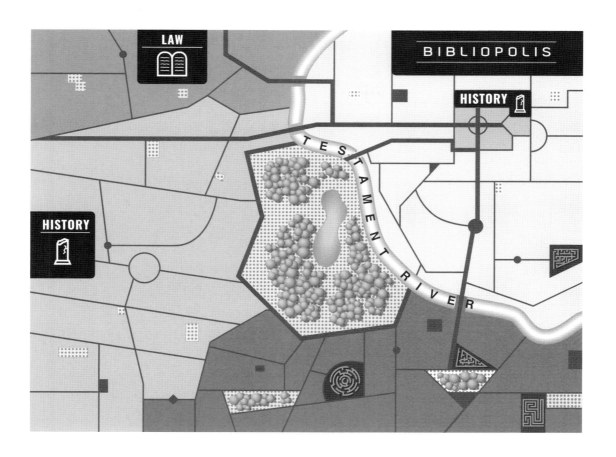

15

POETRY/WISDOM [JOB – SONG OF SOLOMON + LAMENTATIONS]

Writing Style – *Wisdom Literature (Hebrew literary devices and figures of speech)* & *Poetry* that also appear sprinkled throughout the other parts of the Bible

Purpose – Offer guidance, assurance, and warnings on a range of human experiences, including relationships, prosperity, pleasure, praise, and suffering.

 PROPHECY [ISAIAH – MALACHI + REVELATION 4-22]

Writing Style – *Symbolic and Poetic*

Purpose – Describe events many years beyond the date of the writing

Prophecy remains a shadowy maze for many people due to its use of highly figurative language and enigmatic symbols that *do not resemble the things they describe (apocalypse, p. 30).* However, they are some of the most rewarding books once the reader understands the symbolism. They are also critical in affirming the supernatural nature of the Bible by revealing things mere humans could not know or predict.

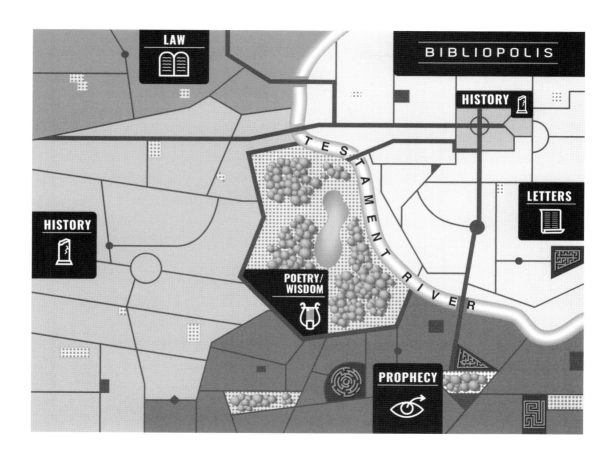

LAW

BIBLIOPOLIS

HISTORY

LETTERS

HISTORY

TESTAMENT RIVER

POETRY/
WISDOM

PROPHECY

17

New Testament River divides the books of the Old Covenant (laws stating how God expects us to live) from the books of the New Covenant (the good news of Jesus fulfilling God's standards on our behalf).

LETTERS [ROMANS TO REVELATION 1-3]

Writing Style – *Prose (plus some symbolic language in Rev. 1-3)*

Purpose – To instruct and encourage Christ-like living and to explain doctrines relating to sin, salvation, and the dual nature of Christ.

....

If we attempt to read all parts of the Bible the same way and do not recognize the distinct writing styles contained in these different locations, we will come to misguided conclusions about what the Bible authors are trying to tell us. So a good first question to ask ourselves is, **"Where am I?"**

WHERE AM I? *[example]*

Here is an example of a preacher who should be familiar with this principle but who is instead teaching an errant reading of a passage because he is ignoring where he is in Scripture (i.e., what kind of literature he is reading):

....

"Jesus didn't show up perfect; He grew into His perfection... And somebody said, 'Well, Jesus came as God!' Well, how do you know? The Bible says **'God never sleeps nor slumbers.'"** And yet, in the book of Mark, we see **Jesus asleep in the back of the boat**...This ain't no heresy. I'm not some false prophet. I'm just reading this thing out to ya out of the Bible." [5]

– Creflo Dollar, Televangelist, World Changers Church International

....

Jesus' identity as God is perhaps *the* central doctrine of our faith. Indeed dismissing it *is* heresy. Dollar attempts to justify his belief that Jesus isn't God by confusing two very different areas of Scripture: Poetry/Wisdom and Letters.

The phrase, *"God never sleeps or slumbers,"* is located in **Psalm 121:4** – an overtly poetic book within Poetry/Wisdom. It is an *anthropomorphism*, a figure of speech ascribing human attributes to God to make His nature more relatable (see "Figures Of Speech," Ch. 3). Verse 3 adds that, *"he will not let your foot slip."* If we read this as Dollar reads verse 4, are we to believe that God will never let us slip on a wet floor? The meaning of this psalm is that God is an omniscient protector who watches over His people. It is not a commentary on His sleeping habits.

However, Jesus asleep in the boat is found in **Mark 4:38**, a book of History. It is a straightforward, prose account of what happened when the disciples had to awaken Jesus when terrified by a sudden squall threatening them on the Sea of Galilee. As God clothed in humanity, His need for physical rest in no way negates any of His Godly attributes. In fact, His response to the storm, a rebuke followed by immediate calm, is a testimony to His Godhood – a refutation of Dollar's original premise.

When faced with passages that appear to conflict, first ask, **"Where am I?,"** and recognize what kind of literature you are reading. Give precedence to passages that are written with straightforward, easily discernible meanings and weigh other less clear passages according to any literary devices they use.

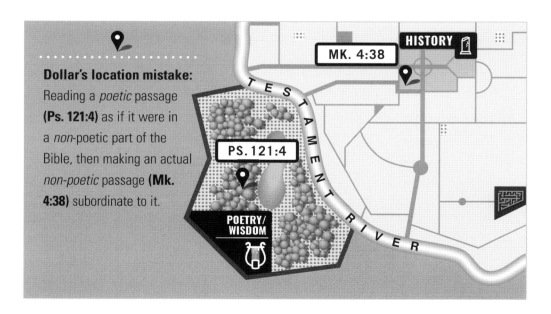

Dollar's location mistake:
Reading a *poetic* passage **(Ps. 121:4)** as if it were in a *non*-poetic part of the Bible, then making an actual *non-poetic* passage **(Mk. 4:38)** subordinate to it.

MK. 4:38

HISTORY

PS. 121:4

TESTAMENT RIVER

POETRY/ WISDOM

ARE THERE ANY FIGURES OF SPEECH?

Sometimes figures of speech are obvious, as in poetic books like Psalms or Proverbs. But other times they can appear amid ordinary language. To better hone in on a passage's meaning we should be able to spot when figures of speech are being used. The more we read, the more familiar we will become with a wide variety of figurative language used in the Bible.

In his 2014 debate with creationist Ken Ham, Bill Nye "the science guy" made the following criticism about Ham's references to Scripture:

"So it sounds to me like you're going to take what you like and interpret **literally**, and other passages you're going to interpret as **poetic**…" [6]

My guess is that even though Bill Nye's area of expertise is science, he still has enough literary instincts not to read a work by Robert Frost or Walt Whitman the same way that he reads a science textbook. Yet, he seems to suspend those same instincts when applied to reading the Bible. He appears unaware that it contains a wide assortment of writing, that, *like any other literary work,* requires the reader to recognize when an author is speaking figuratively or non-figuratively.

The Bible does not always say things in a straightforward manner. Even without reading much of the Bible, just realizing that it has a variety of literature and is loaded with colorful expressions should tell us at least one thing about God — He is *creative*.

He could have given us the information as a dry textbook, but instead He chose to give us a colorful, sophisticated collection of writing that employs the diverse backgrounds, personalities, and writing styles of over forty authors.

For example, in the following verse, Solomon could have merely said that a beautiful woman who behaves indecently ceases to be attractive, but instead he paints a more descriptive (and humorous) picture of just how unattractive she becomes from God's point of view:

> Like a gold ring in a pig's snout is a beautiful woman who shows no discretion.
> — Prov. 11:22

Her indiscretion (the pig) overshadows any beauty (the gold ring) that she has. Consider the figures of speech on the following pages and think about how the mental pictures they create enrich the meaning of what is being said.

SIMILE: A comparison of dissimilar things using *like* or *as*

Like a scarecrow in a melon patch, their idols cannot speak; they must be carried because they cannot walk. — Jer. 10:5

Your enemy the devil prowls around *like* a roaring lion looking for someone to devour. — 1 Pet. 5:8

....

METAPHOR: A comparison of dissimilar things saying one thing *is* another

For the Lord your God *is* a consuming fire, a jealous God. — Prov. 11:22

I *am* the good shepherd. — John 10:11

HYPERBOLE: An intentional exaggeration to emphasize a point

So the Pharisees said to one another, "See, this is getting us nowhere. Look how the *whole world* has gone after him!" — John 12:19

Now I urge you to take some food. You need it to survive. Not one of you will lose *a single hair* from his head." — Acts 27:34

....

METONYMY: Substituting one word for a closely associated word

How beautiful on the mountains are the *feet* of those who bring good news - Isa. 52:7 [*feet* = the site of a welcome messenger]

I will give you the *keys of the kingdom of heaven;* whatever you bind on earth will be bound in heaven... — Matt. 16:19 [*keys* = power]

Your accuser is *Moses,* on whom your hopes are set. — John 5:45 [*Moses* = the Law]

IDIOM: An expression unique to a culture

...He was taken up into heaven and He sat *at the right hand* of God. — Mark 16:19
[*at the right hand* = the position of authority]

From *six* calamities He will rescue you; in *seven* no harm will touch you. — Job 5:19
[*six/seven* = all]

...to bring them up out of that land to a good and broad land, a land *flowing with milk and honey*... — Ex. 3:8
[*flowing with milk and honey* = fertile in livestock and agriculture]

PERSONIFICATION: Ascribing human attributes to something non-human

The *mountains and hills will burst into song*, and the *trees of the field will clap their hands!* — Isa. 55:12

He said, "What have you done? The voice of your brother's *blood is crying to Me from the ground.* — Gen. 4:10

....

ANTHROPOMORPHISM: Ascribing human attributes to God

So the LORD brought us out of Egypt with a *mighty hand and an outstretched arm...* — Deut. 26:8

It is a burnt offering to the LORD, *a pleasing aroma...* — Ex. 29:18

APOCALYPSE: An imaginative, symbolic picture of a future event that has the characteristics but not the appearance of the thing being described

Daniel said, "In my vision at night I looked, and there before me were the four winds of heaven churning up the great sea. "*Four great beasts,* each different from the others, came up out of the sea. The first was *like a lion, and it had the wings of an eagle.* I watched until its wings were torn off and it was *lifted from the ground so that it stood on two feet like a man; and the heart of a man was given to it.* — Dan. 7:2-4
[*winged lion* = Babylonia; *heart of a man* = King Nebuchadnezzar]

....

As we continue through this guide, figures of speech will play a supporting role in properly interpreting other passages we will discuss as well.

WHAT IS THE CONTEXT?

Context is the broader meaning of the text that surrounds and relates to a word, phrase, or passage in question. The meanings of words are not static – they are nuanced by the author's larger point. Reading in context slows us down and allows us to appreciate the big picture of what the author is saying rather than running with a pretext of our own making.

If the three most important factors determining the value of real estate are Location! Location! Location!, then perhaps the most critical factor of interpreting Scripture is,

CONTEXT!

CONTEXT!

CONTEXT!

In my experience, when teaching believers and engaging non-believers about the Bible, probably the most common mistake is reading a passage out of context.

Reading in context does not require an exceptional theological insight. It is simply a matter of taking time to read what the author has put in front of us. Not reading in context is either a sign of a reader's inexperience and/or impatience, or of his/her desire to see his/her preconceptions supported. *Never read a Bible verse in isolation.*

Consider the following examples in which context is critical to discerning the correct meaning:

EXAMPLE #1: Context determines the meaning of *words*

....

And I will give you a new heart, and a new spirit I will put within you. And I will remove the heart of stone from your **flesh** and give you a heart of **flesh**. – Ezek. 36:26

— *vs.* —

For those who live according to the **flesh** set their minds on the things of the **flesh**, but those who live according to the Spirit set their minds on the things of the Spirit. For the mind set on the **flesh** is death, but the mind set on the Spirit is life and peace. – Rom. 8:5-6 *(also Phil. 3:3)*

....

"heart of *stone*"
= **Bad**

"heart of *flesh*"
= **Good**

In the first passage from Ezekiel, the context is that God compares Israel's obstinance (vv. 17–21) with having a "heart of stone" (v. 26). By juxtaposing this against "heart of **flesh**," "flesh" becomes a *positive* metaphor of an obedient heart.

However, in Romans 8, **"flesh"** carries a *negative* connotation (fallen human nature, v. 3) because Paul juxtaposes it against a righteous life led by the Spirit.

 "*flesh*" = **Bad**

"*Spirit*" = **Good**

For a similar example, compare Isa. 14:12 ("morning star" = the evil king of Babylon) to Rev. 22:16 ("morning star" = Jesus).

EXAMPLE #2: Context reveals *figures of speech*

....

> Jesus took bread...broke it and gave it to the disciples, and said, "Take, eat; **this is my body.**" And He took a cup...saying, "Drink of it, all of you, for **this is my blood** of the covenant, which is poured out for many for the forgiveness of sins. – Matt. 26:26-28

....

Although the metaphorical nature of Jesus' words here should be obvious, the Roman Catholic Church infers the doctrine of *transubstantiation* from them – the idea that the bread and wine actually become the body and blood of Christ during Communion.

Let's back up – *why* did Jesus command us to observe Communion? Jesus did not command us to observe Communion to remember the Last Supper – no matter how mystical one attempts to make it. We are commanded to observe Communion so that we will remember His broken body (bread) and shed blood (wine) *on the cross.* Simply put, Communion *points to the crucifixion,* not the Last Supper.

Communion points to **Last Supper** : **Communion** points to **Crucifixion**

Jesus' crucifixion and resurrection – not the consumption of the Messiah's actual body – is *the source* of victorious living and eternal life.

Further, Jesus confirms that the bread and wine are *metaphors* when He plainly recognizes their ordinary nature:

"...I will not drink again of this *fruit of the vine* until that day when I drink it new with you in my Father's kingdom" (v. 29).

The context also includes another metaphor just a few verses later when Jesus refers to Himself as "the shepherd" (v. 31). Certainly He does not intend us to believe that He is a herder of livestock any more than He intends us to believe that He is physically, "the light of the world," "the door," the true vine," etc.

EXAMPLE #3: Context corrects *false doctrine*

"The LORD **brought me forth as the first of His works**, before His deeds of old..." – Prov. 8:22

Jehovah's Witnesses understand the above verse as a proof text to support their preconception that Jesus is a *created* being rather than One who *is* God and was *with* God in the beginning (John 1, Col. 1 & 2, Heb. 1, Rev. 1).

Indeed, the passage has many phrases that sound like something Jesus would say: "My mouth speaks what is true"; "Counsel and sound judgment are mine"; "I love those who love me, and those who seek me find me"; etc. However, a quick glance back to the beginning of the chapter reveals who is speaking – *wisdom* ("Does not *wisdom* call out?," v. 1)

The context is built around a *personification* of wisdom as a *woman* ("her voice," v. 1, "her stand," v. 2, etc.) who gives sound instruction. How can the reader reconcile the feminine pronouns with Jesus?

The passage spells out the figurative nature of the text not only in verse 1 but also in verse 12 ("I, wisdom, dwell together with prudence"). Only by allowing a preconceived, biblically-unsupported notion to drive the reading of the text can one come to the conclusion that Jesus is speaking here.

EXAMPLE #4: Context corrects *assumptions*

....

"And this gospel of the kingdom will be proclaimed **throughout the whole world** as a testimony to all nations, and then the end will come." — Matt. 24:14

....

This example broaches the subject of end-times views which is beyond the scope of this guide. However, one need not appeal to a particular eschatology, but only to the passage itself, in order to make some sense of it.

The context is that after Jesus tells the disciples that the temple will be destroyed, they ask Him, *"... when will these things be, and what will be the sign of your coming and of the close of the age?"* (Matt. 24:3)

A common assumption concerning this passage is that Jesus will not return ("the end") until the gospel is preached to "all nations" (i.e., the entire world). But is this the context Jesus intends His hearers to understand? Jesus lists many things (earthquakes, false prophets, wars, etc.) that have occurred throughout history, so they alone do not identify a specific time frame. However, other references do identify the context of these events.

Phrases such as, "...*you* will hear of wars" (v. 6); "...they will deliver *you* up" (v. 9); '...when *you* see" (v. 15); show that Jesus' intended audience is the disciples to whom He is speaking and their contemporaries.

These verses in addition to culture-specific examples such as, "let those who are *in Judea* flee to the mountains" (v. 16); "let the one who is *in the field* not turn back to take *his cloak*," (v. 18); and fleeing in the "winter or on a *Sabbath*" (v. 20) confirm that "*This generation* will not pass away..." (v. 34), refers to the people living in Jerusalem at that time.

If one attempts to claim that "you" and "this generation" refer to the readers of our present time, then they render Jesus' answer to the disciples meaningless.

But what about the gospel being preached to the "whole world"? The same word for "world" is used elsewhere:

Luke 2:1 – a decree...that *all the world* should be registered
Acts 11:28 – Agabus...foretold... a great famine over *all the world*
Acts 24:5 – "[Paul]... one who stirs up riots among all the Jews *throughout the world*" [7]

"the **whole world**"

"the **whole world**"

In each example, the context clearly indicates that "world" means the Mediterranean nations (i.e., Roman Empire), not the entire globe. Likewise, given His use of pronouns for His immediate audience and the time-specific cultural references, Jesus' meaning is that the gospel will be preached to the Roman-controlled world before the "end comes," i.e., the destruction of Israel in 70 A.D. that will cause all who listened to Him to flee Jerusalem.

EXAMPLE #5: Context corrects *radical eisegesis*

...who, although He existed in the form of God, did not regard equality with God a thing to be grasped, but **emptied Himself**, taking the form of a bond-servant, and being made in the likeness of men. – Phil. 2:6–7 (NASB)

As you recall, *eisegesis* means reading preconceived notions into the Bible. I can think of no better example than the following explanation of the previous verses by progressive creationist Hugh Ross:

....

"In coming to Earth as an embryo in the virgin's womb, Christ 'emptied' Himself leaving behind the extra-dimensional realm and capacities He shared with God the Father and God the Holy Spirit. When He had completed the work He set out to do, the work of redemption, He returned to the place and powers He had left behind." *– Beyond The Cosmos* [8]

....

What Ross means is that Jesus temporarily emptied Himself of His divine attributes ("capacities") when He came to earth as a human being and regained them once returning to heaven. His mention of the "extra-dimensional realm" comes from his reliance on the highly theoretical (and completely unobserved) concept of String

Theory, which he believes indicates eleven dimensions of existence:

"He could experience suffering and death in **all the human-occupied dimensions** and then transition into any of His other dimensions or realms once the atonement price had been paid."

– Beyond The Cosmos [9]

The theological flaws in Ross' interpretation are serious, but since this chapter concerns context rather than doctrine, I will address those flaws in the next chapter.

One need only to study the context to rightly discern the meaning of Philippians 2. Paul's exhortation in the first few verses is that believers should imitate Christ's humility by doing nothing out of conceit or self interest because Jesus Himself took on the form of a servant and *"humbled Himself...to the point of death"* (v. 7–8)!

I think its safe to conclude that Paul had servanthood, not string theory, in mind here. Within the context of humility, the sense in which Christ "emptied Himself" was that He relinquished the *benefits* of Godhood (its glory) – not its *attributes*. *"He did not regard equality with God a thing to be grasped,"* means that Christ did not hold onto the glory of Godhood but exchanged it for the humiliation of human suffering.

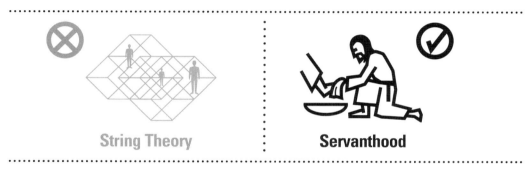

String Theory   **Servanthood**

Jesus *never* loses any Godly attributes – to do so would be a change in His nature. He is eternally, fully God (Mal. 3:6, Col. 1:19 & 2:9, James 1:17, Heb. 13:8). And even if we accepted that He left behind His "extra-dimensional capacities," how then would He return "to the place and powers He had left behind" without relying on those same capacities of which He "emptied" Himself? [10]

DOES **DOCTRINE** SUPPORT IT?

Doctrines are the guard rails that keep our interpretation of the Bible theologically valid. They are the immovable, non-negotiable principles expressed in Scripture – whether explicitly or implicitly – that make Christianity *Christian*. If we ignore a doctrine when determining the meaning of a passage then we risk leading ourselves and others astray.

Generally speaking, a teaching in the Bible is considered doctrine if it is:

1) **Explicitly spelled out** in Scripture in more than one place.
   E.g. – The doctrine that *Jesus is God* is communicated in unambiguous language in John 1, Col. 1 & 2, Heb. 1, and Rev. 1, among other passages.

2) **Implicitly supported by multiple passages** that communicate the same message.
   E.g. – The doctrine of the *Trinity* is not explicitly stated in the Bible, but Matt. 3:16–17, John 6:27, John 8:58, and Acts 5:3–4 and other passages make it evident that the Father, Son, and Holy Spirit are co-equal, co-existent, and co-eternally God.

We should not elevate *one verse in isolation* to the level of doctrine.

Some fundamental Biblical doctrines include: there is only one God; Jesus is God; man has a sinful nature; salvation is by faith, not works; Satan is an actual being; etc. Unambiguous doctrines such as these are the foundation for interpreting Scripture passages that are less clear.

EXAMPLE #1: Doctrine resists *radical eisegesis*

Here again is an excerpt from Hugh Ross regarding how he believes Jesus paid for the sin of mankind:

....

> "He could experience suffering and death in all the human-occupied dimensions and then transition into any of His other dimensions or realms once the **atonement** price had been paid."
>
> — *Beyond The Cosmos* [11]

....

The doctrine in question is the **atonement** — the death of Jesus on the cross that was sufficient to pay the penalty of sinners, satisfy the justice of God, and reunite with God all who believe in Jesus' sacrifice.

Ross can't resist the temptation to explain everything in terms of physics — even the divine. The problem is that in the above statement his misapplied scientific speculation does significant harm to the foundational doctrine of the atonement. His statement raises the question: is a one-to-one, life-for-life sacrifice by a

Messiah necessary to reconcile each individual to God? The answer is found in Scripture (not a physics book), and that answer is an emphatic *no*. Jesus' *single* death due to His impeccable righteousness was sufficient to pay for *all sinners in all times:*

> For Christ also *suffered once for sins*, the righteous for the unrighteous, that He might bring us to God. — 1 Pet. 3:18 (also Rom. 6:10 and Heb. 9:28)

The concept of multiple deaths in multiple dimensions, if not heretical, is at the very least outside the bounds of Scripture.

....

Several controversial books by professing believers have come out in the last few years that highlight the critical need for understanding doctrine. Although these books have been addressed in total by other books, I want to examine a couple of excerpts to highlight the critical role doctrine plays in preserving Scripture.

EXAMPLE #2: Doctrine refutes *human-centered thinking*

The following is from Rob Bell's book, *Love Wins:*

....

"If the message of Jesus is that God is offering the free gift of eternal life through him – a gift that we cannot earn by our own efforts, works or good deeds – and all we have to do is accept and confess and believe, aren't those verbs? And aren't verbs actions? Accepting, confessing, believing – **those are things we do**. Does that mean then, that going to heaven is dependent on something I do? **How is any of that Grace? How is that a gift? How is that Good News?"** – *Love Wins* [12]

....

In the context of Bell's book, accepting, confessing, and believing are *works* a loving God would not require people to do, and therefore, heaven is for everyone.

Saving **"work"** (Bell) Saving **"work"** (Jesus)

Jesus' sacrificial death apparently ensures salvation whether a person believes in it or not. Others have already repudiated[13] this heresy comprehensively, so I'll just allow a couple of plainly stated Bible passages to suffice as the argument:

> Whoever believes in Him is not condemned, but *whoever does not believe stands condemned already* because they have not believed in the name of God's one and only Son. — John 3:18

> "Then *they will go away to eternal punishment,* but the righteous to eternal life." — Matt. 25:46

If someone gives me a Christmas gift and I leave it on the floor and walk away, I not only fail to receive any benefit from the gift, but I also insult the giver. Too complicated? Apparently so.

Scripture is clear about the gospel that Bell seems intent on confusing. Are faith and belief considered to be *works?* Jesus answers this way:

> Then they said to Him, "What must we do, to be doing the works of God?" Jesus answered them, "This is the *work* of God, that you *believe* in Him whom He has sent." — John 6:28–29

Is Jesus using "work" in a one-dimensional sense or is this a *figure of speech?* It is the latter. The *context* is that Jesus has told the crowd not to, "work for food that spoils" (i.e., physical effort). They respond by asking what "works" (physical effort) they can do to please God.

As He often does, Jesus answers people in their owns words but pours new spiritual meaning into those words (see, "Why do you call me *good?*" - Mark 10:18). For Jesus, the "work of God" means belief (faith) *in the work He does,* not performing acts of physical effort (action verbs).

Paul clarifies this doctrine by clearly setting faith apart from works in Eph. 2:8–9:

> For by grace you have been saved through *faith*. And this is not your own doing; it is the gift of God, not a result of *works*, so that no one may boast.

Paul further distinguishes the two in Eph. 2:10:

> For we are His workmanship, created in Christ Jesus *for* good works...

We are saved *for* good works (i.e., *in order to do* good works). Works come *after* salvation, making them distinct from faith and belief, which come *before* salvation. Due to our sinful nature, nothing is counted as a good work until we are given a new nature *("created in Christ")* that empowers us to perform it.

EXAMPLE #3: Doctrine refutes *emotional storytelling*

You know when you board a plane and look down the aisle and see that two-thirds of the people on the flight are reading the same book, and that book purports to be a *Christian book,* then it's time to be suspicious (1 Cor. 2:14, Jer. 6:10).

So it was for me several years ago not long after I had heard about William P. Young's *The Shack,* a novel that quickly became a huge bestseller (over 20 million copies sold to date). A 2017 Hollywood film of the same title based on the book brought it back into the spotlight, further impressing the problematic theological footprints upon the popular culture.

The story is about a main character named Mack who, after experiencing the devastating loss of his daughter, has a weekend-long conversation in a shack with an unconventional *trinity* represented by a large black woman ("Papa" – the Father), a Middle-Eastern man (Jesus – the Son), and a small Asian woman ("Sarayu" – the Holy Spirit).

Mack is able to converse with each character face-to-face, frankly and intimately, so that the reader is not only immersed in the story but also instructed in spiritual matters by this trio as Mack is. The result is a reader who becomes emotionally attached but theologically misguided by the spiritual guidance given.

Yes, as a graphic designer, writer, and speaker, I do appreciate artistic license and especially symbolism, but one should exercise caution regarding where that license is applied. Perhaps depicting God and putting words in His mouth in a fictional setting is the point at which the author/artist should heed the second Commandment or at least the words of legendary graphic designer Paul Rand: *"Don't try to be original, just try to be good."*

The overarching doctrine in question here is **God's self-revelation**. I'll briefly address just two issues relating to this doctrine that *The Shack* misrepresents: *1)* God's identity, and *2)* the relationship of the members of the Trinity.

1) God's identity

It's curious that Young depicts two of the three members of the Trinity as female. He puts the reasoning for this in the mouth of Papa:

> "Mackenzie, I am **neither male nor female**, even though both genders are derived from my nature. If I choose to appear to you as a man or a woman, it's because I love you." [14]

Although it is true that both male and female are made in the image of God (Gen. 1:27), *God never reveals His persona as anything but male*, so Young has no biblical reason to do otherwise. Due to man's fallen nature, *we only know about God what He chooses to reveal to us*. Therefore, we have no license to depict Him in any way other than how He depicts Himself, even if our intentions are good.

Throughout Scripture *all* pronouns for each member of the Trinity are masculine ("He," "Him,"). *All* titles and designations when a gender is indicated are masculine

("Father," "Son," "king," "groom," "husband"). Some dispute this by citing passages in which feminine comparisons are made to God:

"As a *mother* comforts her child, so will I comfort you…" — Isa. 66:13

"Like a bear robbed of *her* cubs, I will attack them…" — Hos. 13:8

"…how often I have longed to gather your children together, as a *hen* gathers *her* chicks…" — Matt. 23:37

However, each of these are *similes* (p. 25) designed to describe situational *actions,* not define *identity*. Obviously God has no gender in the human sense (John 4:24), but when having the choice to identity Himself as one of the two sexes, He always chooses male. This is a matter of *revelation,* not chauvinism. Depicting God in any other way violates the second Commandment — worshiping the right God the wrong way.

2) The relationship of the members of the Trinity

The Trinity is a difficult and mysterious subject, and although we can't completely comprehend it, there are some things Scripture reveals about it to us. Young again takes a puzzling position when describing how the members of the Trinity relate to each other:

> "Mackenzie, we have no concept of final authority among us, only unity. We are in a circle of relationship, not a chain of command... **Hierarchy would make no sense** among us."
>
> "Papa is as much submitted to me as I to him, or Sarayu to me, or Papa to her. Submission is not about authority and it is not obedience; it's all about relationships of love and respect. In fact, we are **submitted to you** in the same way." [15]

Young is right that submission within the Godhead involves love and respect.

However, he is wrong that it does not involve authority and obedience. Consider the following verses regarding these two attributes within the Trinity:

The Son *submits* to the Father:

> "For I have come down from heaven, *not to do my own will but the will of Him who sent me.*" — John 6:38

> "*I do nothing on my own authority*, but speak just as the Father taught me." — John 8:28

> ...*the Son Himself will also be subjected to Him* who put all things in subjection under Him... — 1 Cor. 15:28

The Holy Spirit *submits* to the Father and the Son:

> "And *I will ask the Father, and He will give you* another Helper, to be with you forever..." — John 14:16

"When the Spirit of truth comes...*He will not speak on His own authority,* but whatever He hears He will speak... *He will glorify me,* for He will take what is mine and declare it to you." – John 14:16

Although, Jesus nor the Holy Spirit act on their own authority in these passages, this does not make them less than God. Living out perfect obedience is as Godly as living out perfect authority. Although the Father takes a lead *role* in carrying out His plan on Earth, each Person of the Trinity is equal to the others in essence. Each of the three have an equally critical cooperative role in the redemption of sinners: the Father *initiates* salvation; the Son *secures* it; and the Holy Spirit *applies* it. [16]

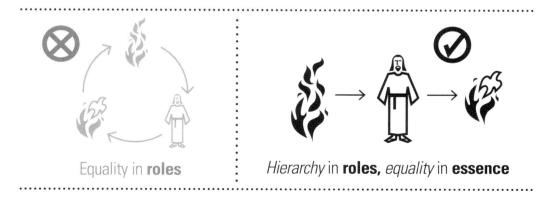

Equality in **roles**

Hierarchy in **roles,** *equality* in **essence**

As for the comment that, *"...we are submitted to you in the same way."* I can't think of any theological concept more nonsensical or backward. *Nowhere in Scripture* does transcendent, holy God submit His will to fallen man's will:

> "For as the heavens are higher than the earth, so are my ways higher than your ways and my thoughts than your thoughts." — Isa. 55:9

> "...*you thought that I was one like yourself.* But now I rebuke you and lay the charge before you." — Ps. 50:21

In his zeal to present God as tender and sympathetic, Young has unfortunately put misleading instructions for a biblically illiterate culture into the mouth of a god of his own making.

DO OTHER PASSAGES AGREE?

It is easy for a reader to find a single verse to back up a belief that he or she may already hold. However, Bible verses don't exist alone. They express ideas that may develop throughout many areas of Scripture. Before we deduce a passage's meaning, we may need to consult other passages in which the idea in question occurs.

A great question to ask ourselves when confronting a difficult passage is, *"Does this author or another refer to this subject elsewhere in the Bible?"* Today it is easier than ever to cross-reference a passage due to the ability to search specific words in e-bibles.

In this chapter, we will put together all five of the key questions to determine the meaning of a difficult passage with weighty theological significance:

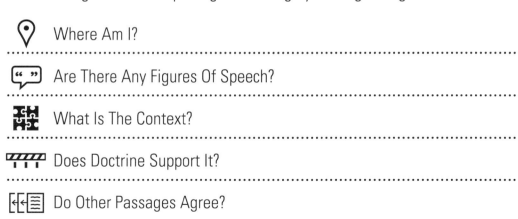

Where Am I?

Are There Any Figures Of Speech?

What Is The Context?

Does Doctrine Support It?

Do Other Passages Agree?

The passage in question, **Matt. 27:46** (also Mark 15:34), is one that in my own teaching and speaking experience has inclined people to latch onto an interpretation based on what they've *heard* rather than on what they've *read* in Scripture. Here is the verse :

And at the ninth hour Jesus cried with a loud voice, "Eloi, Eloi, lema sabachthani?" which means, "My God, my God, **why have you forsaken me?"** – Matt. 27:46

How are we to understand Jesus' cry from the cross? There is clear theological tension created by one Person of the Trinity being separated from ("forsaken" by) the others. Does the doctrine of the atonement require a presumed divine schism? Let's first look at the most common explanation of this passage, what I'm calling the "*Separation* Interpretation," and then compare it to an alternate explanation, the "*Imputation* Interpretation," by seeing what other passages have to say.

EXPLANATION #1: The *Separation* Interpretation

The diagram on the next page shows the verses along with their perceived interpretations that are usually pulled together to support this explanation. I will describe several problems with this and then offer an alternate explanation:

(1) **MATT. 27:46** — Jesus' cry, *"...why have you forsaken me,"* is commonly explained as God "turning His back" on Jesus. I've heard this repeated so often in evangelical churches that it seems to have taken on Scriptural authority. The idea has even been popularized in Stuart Townend's hymn, "How Deep The Father's Love For Us."* The problem is that Scripture doesn't support it.

 Other Passages — Jesus taught that the Father would always be with Him:

"Behold, the hour is coming, indeed it has come, when you will be scattered, each to his own home, and will leave me alone. *Yet I am not alone, for the Father is with me.*" — John 16:32 (also John 8:28-29)

* "How deep the pain of searing loss / The Father turns His face away"

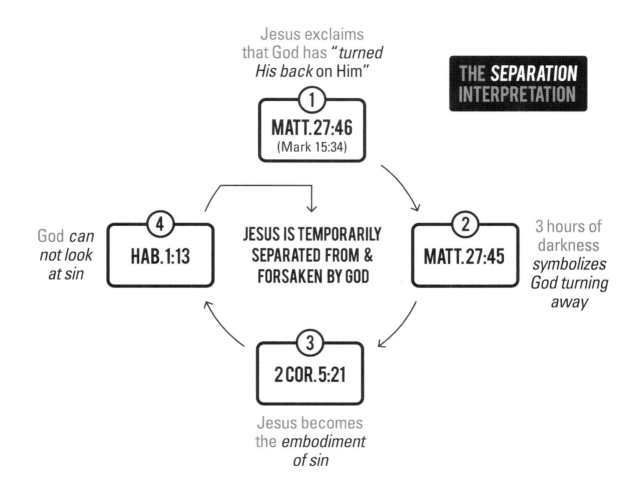

THE **SEPARATION** INTERPRETATION

Jesus exclaims that God has *"turned His back on Him"*

1 MATT. 27:46
(Mark 15:34)

3 hours of darkness *symbolizes God turning away*

2 MATT. 27:45

Jesus becomes the *embodiment of sin*

3 2 COR. 5:21

God *can not look at sin*

4 HAB. 1:13

JESUS IS TEMPORARILY SEPARATED FROM & FORSAKEN BY GOD

This is a direct reference to the time in which the disciples will abandon Jesus when He goes to the cross. However, Jesus assures them that the Father will be with Him. (The Greek word means the Father's *ongoing* presence.) [17]

---

② **MATT. 27:45** – *How do we know* the 3 hours of darkness symbolize God turning away (Matt. 27:45)? Do any other passages support this? *No.*

Other Passages – Throughout the O.T. celestial darkness symbolizes God's judgment (e.g., Joel 2:2). The most closely related passage to the description of darkness at the crucifixion is in Amos 8:

> "And on that day," declares the Lord GOD, "I will make the *sun go down at noon* and darken the earth in broad daylight." – Amos 8:9

> "...I will make it *like the mourning for an only son* and the end of it like a bitter day." – Amos 8:10

These verses predict God's Old Testament judgment of Israel for their rebellion. If applied in a similar way, the darkness at Jesus' crucifixion could symbolize God's coming judgment of Israel (via Rome) for murdering the Messiah.

In any case, no direct explanation is given, and there is no suggestion in Scripture that darkness indicates God turning away from those He judges.

....

(3) **2 COR. 5:21** — This is the pivotal verse for this interpretation:

> For our sake He *made Him to be sin* who knew no sin, so that in Him we might become the righteousness of God. — 2 Cor. 5:21

Doctrine — The argument is that Jesus *became sin* on the cross (as if sin were a physical thing), or that His nature transformed into one consisting of all human sin. However, this is a strange idea in light of fundamental doctrine.

As already discussed, first and foremost, *Jesus is God.* Less clear details surrounding His nature should be assessed in light of explicit passages such as John 1, Col. 1 & 2, Heb. 1, and Rev. 1. His temporarily taking on human flesh (1 Tim. 3:16) and "bearing" of mankind's sin (1 Pet. 2:24) on the cross *in no way compromises His perfect, eternal nature:*

> Jesus Christ is *the same yesterday and today and forever.* — Heb. 13:8

> "For I the LORD *do not change..."* — Mal. 3:6

The very reason we should be unchangeable in our faith is because the character/ nature of Christ *does not ever change* according to Heb. 13:8. This would include Jesus' time on the cross.

If God does not change, and Jesus is the embodiment of God:

> For in Him the *whole fullness of deity dwells bodily...* — Col. 2:9

...and God has no sin in Him:

God is light, and *in Him is no darkness at all.* — I John 1:5

...then Jesus *can not ever have any sin in Him,* much less embody the sin of mankind:

> You know that He appeared *to take away sins,* and *in Him there is no sin.* — 1John 3:5

Further, if Jesus lived a sinless life then suddenly "became sin" on the cross, He would no longer be qualified to pay for the sin of mankind! Only an *unblemished* sacrifice is able to pay for sin:

> ...how much more will the blood of Christ, who through the eternal Spirit *offered Himself without blemish to God*, purify our conscience from dead works to serve the living God. — Heb. 9:14 (also 1 Pet. 1:19)

Jesus went sinless to the cross and remained that way. We will unpack how Jesus actually *bore* mankind's sin in Explanation #2.

(4) HAB. 1:13 — Does Habakkuk say that God is too pure to look at sin? Only if you read the verse out of context.

Context — Advocates of this view only cite the first half of Hab. 1:13 to support this idea:

> You who are of *purer eyes than to see evil and cannot look at wrong,*...

...but the second half clarifies the meaning:

> ...why do you *idly look at traitors* and *remain silent when the wicked swallows up* the man more righteous than he? — Hab. 1:13

Habakkuk clearly says that *God does look on sin* but remains silent. The context of Habakkuk's complaint is that God can not look on sin *with approval* ("...idly look...").* He doesn't understand how God can use an evil nation (Babylon) to judge Israel and yet appear unwilling to judge Babylon's evil as well.

*See also Prov. 15:3 and Jer. 16:17.

"...My God, my God, **why have you forsaken me?**" – Matt. 27:46

....

EXPLANATION #2: The *Imputation* Interpretation (diagram next page)

I believe this explanation is far more biblical than the preceding one. *Imputation* is the term used to describe Christ's righteousness that is credited to us (i.e., put into our account). Imputation is a cornerstone of salvation.

① **MATT. 27:46** – Does a one-dimensional reading of this verse conflict with what we already know about Jesus? *Yes.*

▨▨ **Doctrine** – Jesus and the Father (and the Holy Spirit) are eternally *one.*

"I and the Father *are one.*" – John 10:30

"Hear, O Israel: The LORD our God,* the LORD *is one.*" – Deut. 6:4

*The word for "God" is plural in this verse, indicating a unity of Persons.

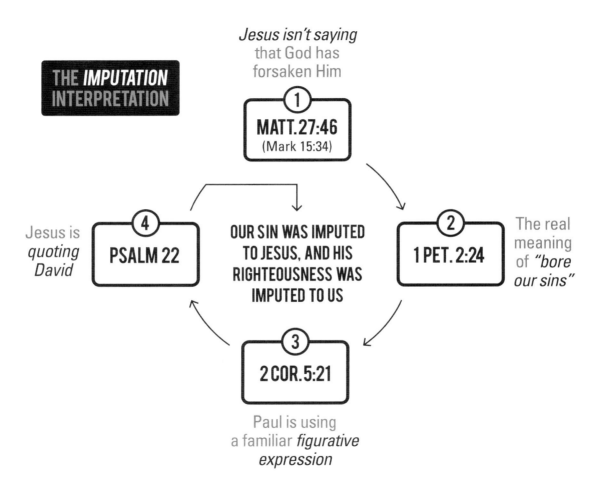

THE *IMPUTATION* INTERPRETATION

Jesus isn't saying that God has forsaken Him

①
MATT.27:46
(Mark 15:34)

②
1 PET. 2:24

The real meaning of *"bore our sins"*

③
2 COR.5:21

Paul is using a familiar *figurative expression*

④
PSALM 22

Jesus is *quoting* David

OUR SIN WAS IMPUTED TO JESUS, AND HIS RIGHTEOUSNESS WAS IMPUTED TO US

▟▟▟ **Doctrine** – As repeated already in this guide, numerous passages plainly affirm that Jesus is fully God. He could not "become sin" any more than the Father or the Holy Spirit could.

⋯⋯⋯

② **1 PET. 2:24** – Perhaps the idea that Jesus' body became the physical manifestation of sin on the cross comes from this verse:

He himself *bore our sins in His body* on the tree, that we might die to sin and live to righteousness. – 1 Pet. 2:24 (also Isa. 53:11)

🗨 **Figures Of Speech** – In what sense did Jesus *bear* our sins in His body? The verb "bear" can be taken a couple of different ways: *1)* "to hold or remain firm under (a load;)" or *2)* "give birth to." I don't think most people who read this verse believe that Jesus gave birth to our sins, but I do think many believe that He bore them by somehow taking them into His body.

However, the Greek word for "bore" in 1 Pet. 2:24 is *anaphero,* meaning: "to carry or bring up, to lead up / [lead] men to a higher place / to put upon the altar, to bring to the altar, to offer." [18]

This definition helps clarify what is happening on the cross. Rather than Jesus absorbing our sins into Himself and becoming the physical manifestation of sin, He *carries His own body to the cross bearing the weight (liability) of our sin* just as a priest would carry to the altar an unblemished sacrificial animal bearing the weight of the Israelites' sins. Jesus is both the *high priest* and the *unblemished sacrifice* (Heb. 7:26–27). (For a similar situation, see Num. 14:33.*) [19]

Jesus **embodies** sin

Jesus **bears the burden** of sin

*The second generation of desert Israelites are liable for their parents' unfaithfulness.

③ **2 COR. 5:21** – In the discussion of this verse in the "Separation Interpretation" we saw that doctrine opposes the idea that Jesus actually embodied sin while on the cross. Is there a clue in the verse that we should read it another way? I think so. Here again is the verse:

For our sake He made Him to be sin who knew no sin, so that *in Him* we might become the righteousness of God. – 2 Cor. 5:21

💬 **Figures Of Speech** – There are no overt, poetic figures of speech in this verse, but there is a figurative expression that Paul uses frequently, "in Him." It means that *our nature and identity are overshadowed by and hidden within His.*

In other words, Paul does not mean that we physically embody the righteousness of God. If we did, upon being saved we would not sin anymore. Rather, we are counted positionally/legally righteous because Christ's righteousness is *credited* (imputed) to us even though we continue to sin (Rom. 4:23).

The two halves of 2 Cor. 5:21 are counterparts describing an exchange of moral capital on the cross: Jesus' righteousness was *credited to us* (we "became righteousness") in the same way that our sin was *credited to Him* (He "became sin"):

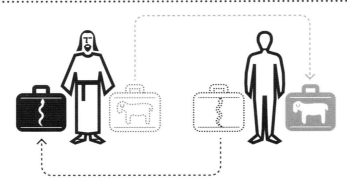

Our sin debt is **exchanged** for Jesus' righteousness

Isaiah 53:12 says that Jesus was, "*numbered with* the transgressors," (i.e., credited with transgressions) not that he became a transgressor.

Other Passages – Is there another passage that sheds some light on the meaning of 2 Cor. 21? *Yes.* Paul himself does this in Rom. 8:3:

> ...by sending His own Son in the likeness of sinful flesh to be a *sin offering*.
> — Rom. 8:3 (NASB, NIV) (also Isa. 53:10)

In this verse Paul makes it clear that Jesus was a *sin offering* – not sin incarnate. *Sin* can not pay the price for *sin* – only an unblemished sacrifice can (Heb. 9:14).

. . . .

(4) **PSALM 22** – Is Jesus' cry from the cross the first time these words have been uttered in Scripture? *No.*

Context – It is amazing to me that as many times as I've heard the "Separation Interpretation," I've never heard someone defending it mention the most critical aspect of Matt. 27:46 – that *Jesus is quoting the Old Testament*.

"My God, my God, why have you forsaken me? Why are you so far from saving me, from the words of my groaning?"* — Ps. 22:1

Jesus always quotes Scripture in perfect context;* therefore, considering the Providential similarities between Psalm 22 and Matt. 27:46, we first need to look at the context of Psalm 22 in order to interpret Matt. 27:46.

Jesus is **quoting David**

*See Jesus' answers from Deut. 8:2–3 and 6:13–16 to Satan. He is being tested after forty days in the desert, so He selects passages describing Israel being tested forty years in the desert.

David wrote Psalm 22 to express the anguish of being pursued by his enemies. However, his words uncannily describe what sounds like a *crucifixion* — specifically, Jesus' crucifixion — that would not occur until a thousand years later!:

> *"...all my bones are out of joint*; my heart is like wax; it is melted within my breast..."* — Ps. 22:14

> *"...my tongue sticks to my jaws..."* — Ps. 22:15

> *"... a company of evildoers encircles me; they have pierced my hands and feet..."* — Ps. 22:16

> *"... they stare and gloat over me; they divide my garments among them, and for my clothing they cast lots."* — Ps. 22:17–18

*The strain of being on the cross could cause the shoulder and elbow joints to dislocate.[20]

Psalm 22 is *not* about being separated from God as a result of one's sin. It is about calling on God while being oppressed or attacked. Further, its full context reveals where God is in the midst of this trial. Verse 24 says:

> "For He has *not despised or abhorred* the affliction of the afflicted, and *He has not hidden His face from Him,* but has heard, when He cried to Him." — Ps. 22:24

In verse 24, David (foreshadowing Jesus) is "the afflicted." He follows up his painful expressions by proclaiming his assurance that God *has not turned away* from him (i.e., "turned His back") – directly disputing the core idea of the "Separation Interpretation."

Jews witnessing the crucifixion would have been familiar with Psalm 22. (Since chapters and verses were not assigned until much later, people quoted the first line of a passage to identify it.) I believe Jesus quotes this passage because He wants the crowd to recognize that He is the ultimate subject of David's prophetic psalm and the promised King from the line of David. (This is a *typology* – a person, place, thing, or event in the Old Testament that foreshadows and finds fulfillment in a spiritual truth in the New Testament. There is much to be said about typologies, but that will have to wait for a future book.)

In conclusion, if we read the entire psalm, we will see in verse 24 that David, and therefore, Jesus, is *not abandoned*. God is silent, not absent.

MOVING FORWARD

Hopefully you've discovered that reading the Bible "literally" requires the same kinds of tools as reading any other literary work. This realization should be both a comfort and a challenge.

In my experience teaching and speaking, I think that many people approaching the Bible leave their reading skills at the door for one of two reasons: 1) They have already judged it to be outdated, unreal, and irrelevant, so they rely on hearsay rather than first-hand experience; or 2) They are so familiar with it from being in church all of their lives that they rely only on what they've always heard rather than really examining what has been written.

Many times after asking a group (students and adults alike) a question about a passage, someone will look up and recite a rote, general answer without looking *down* to the Book and referencing the passage we've just read.

A healthy approach lies somewhere between being jaded from unfamiliarity and being jaded from over-familiarity. Of course being familiar with the Bible is great, but we should learn to *read it* rather than reading *over* it through the lens of the same old expectations and assumptions. Doing this means that we can always glean something new from the multi-faceted nature of Scripture.

Moving forward, read a passage as if you've never read it before, and let it speak for itself through whatever devices the Spirit has inspired the authors to use. Take note of how both the message and the means that convey the message say something about God. In doing so, Scripture will become more real and memorable.

END NOTES

What Does "Literally" Mean?
1. Bryant, Dewayne. M.A.. "The Bible's Buried Secrets." Accessed 12 Aug. 2016.
<http://www.apologeticspress.org/apcontent.aspx?category=13&article=2753>

2. Fleming, Reneé. The 38th Annual Kennedy Center Honors. Television broadcast. 29 Dec. 2015.

3. Puig, Claudia. "Spiritual Carrey Still Mighty Funny." USA Today Online. 20 May 2003
<http://www.usatoday.com/life/2003-05-20-carrey_x.htm>

4. Mortenson, Terry Ph. D. and Thane Ury Ph. D. "Coming To Grips With Genesis." Green Forest, AR: Master Books. 2009. 318–319 p.

Where Am I?
5. MacArthur, John. "Declaring And Defending The Deity Of Christ." 14 Oct., 2012.
http://www.gty.org/resources/sermons/43-1/declaring-and-defending-the-deity-of-christ
Video of this quote here: https://www.youtube.com/watch?v=0vkeVhQo7MY
Clear audio here: https://www.youtube.com/watch?v=-NV1plklvhg

Are There Any Figures Of Speech?
6. Browning, Bill. "Transcript of Ken Ham vs Bill Nye Debate." 10 Feb. 2014.
<http://www.youngearth.org/index.php/archives/rmcf-articles/item/21-transcript-of-ken-ham-vs-bill-nye-debate>

What Is The Context?

7. Storms, Sam. *Kingdom Come*. Scotland, UK: Mentor. 2013. pp. 242–244 p.

8. Craig, William L. "Hugh Ross's Extra-Dimensional Diety." Philosophia Christi. 13 Nov. 13 1999. Accessed 12 Aug. 2016.; <http://www.reasons.org/articles/philosophia-christi#heading3>

9. Ibid.

10. Ibid.

Does Doctrine Support It?

11. Ibid.

12. Bell, Rob. *Love Wins*. Harper Collins e-books. 2011. Accessed 12 Aug. 2016. <https://books.google.com/books?id=WclJcNFzgqgC&printsec=frontcover&dq=love+wins&hl=en&sa=X-&ved=0ahUKEwiSjc29gb3OAhXJKB4KHXD2CqoQ6AEIKjAC#v=onepage&q=love%20wins&f=false>

13. Sources repudiating Bell's theology in *Love Wins*:
Chan, Francis and Preston Sprinkle. *Erasing Hell*. Colorado Springs, CO: David C. Cook. 2011.

Mohler, Albert. "We Have Seen All This Before: Rob Bell and the (Re)Emergence of Liberal Theology." 16 Mar. 2011. <http://www.albertmohler.com/2011/03/16/we-have-seen-all-this-before-rob-bell-and-the-re-emergence-of-liberal-theology/>

Parnell, Jonathan. "God: Abounding in Love, Punishing the Guilty." 14 Apr. 2011. <http://www.desiringgod.org/articles/god-abounding-in-love-punishing-the-guilty>

14. Challies, Tim. "A Reader's Review of the Shack." PDF document. Jan. 2008. 15 p.

15. Mohler, Albert. "The Shack – The Missing Art of Evangelical Discernment." 27 Jan. 2010. Accessed 12 Aug. 2016.; <http://www.albertmohler.com/2010/01/27/the-shack-the-missing-art-of-evangelical-discernment/>

Do Other Passages Agree?
16. Lawson, Steven. "God's Sovereignty in Salvation and the Unity of the Trinity." 11 May 2015. Accessed 13 Aug. 2016.; <http://www.ligonier.org/blog/gods-sovereignty-salvation-and-unity-trinity/>

17. *anaphero.* Lexicon : Strong's G399. Accessed 13 Aug. 2016. <https://www.blueletterbible.org/lang/lexicon/lexicon.cfm?Strongs=G399&t=KJV>

18. *esti.* Lexicon : Strong's G399. Accessed 13 Aug. 2016. <https://www.blueletterbible.org/lang/lexicon/lexicon.cfm?Strongs=G399&t=KJV>
and
Keating, Corey. "Greek Verb Tenses." Accessed 13 Aug. 2016. <http://www.ntgreek.org/learn_nt_greek/inter-tense.htm>

19. Ellicott, Charles. "1 Peter 2:24." Ellicott's Commentary for English Readers. Accessed 13 Aug. 2016. <http://biblehub.com/commentaries/ellicott/1_peter/2.htm>

20. Terasaka, David M.D. "Medical Aspects of the Crucifixion of Jesus Christ." 1996. <https://www.blueletterbible.org/comm/terasaka_david/misc/crucify.cfm>